Sun Shine Poems

Sun Shine Poems

Written by: Doris Mesing

John Bo Mesing

Contents

Contents

This book is dedicated to my beloved husband,
who always took such good care of me
(even in my highest and darkest hours)
and the treasures of my life, my six children

About the Author

SunShine Poems by Doris Mesing will most certainly warm your heart. This small book of SunShine poems was written by a mother of six children. Doris was a registered nurse for a few years but ended up as a stay-at-home mom as her family grew from three and four to eight including her beloved husband, John. Doris was active in church, with girl scouts, in the neighborhood, with her six children, and with her writing. She wore her feelings on her sleeve, and never hesitated to share what was going through her mind - and sometimes it was jaw-dropping! Enjoy these poems, her love, and her gratitude. These loving poems share a glimpse of Doris Mesing's heart from the '60s into the '80s. Enjoy her poems and stories that include a wide range of precious stars from her beloved children and husband to the butterfly lady, the janitor, the girl scout stories, the football prayer, the crimson lady (a volunteer worker), living in paradise, the holidays and more, ending with her prayer and thanks to God for all she lived.

1

To Sandy with Love

I wrote this for my daughter Sandy,
in June of 1970 for her high school graduation day.

Today is very special,
your graduation day;
And I want to tell you what you mean to me
in every little way.

I remember when you were born,
how much I loved you;
You were such a happy baby,
my, how fast you grew.

I remember the ponytail,
then brownies and girl scouts came;
Time went so quickly
family picnics — things are still the same.

I went to the hospital many times,
and you had to grow up fast;
You were like a little mother

and helped much in the past.

Sunday school and church were a must,
and you learned how to pray;
God was always watching over you,
even as He is guiding you today.

You went to work at the tobacco farm,
and that was hard indeed;
But I was so proud of you,
you bought some school clothes you would need.

As you grew older
clothes were a very special thing;
You worked as a tray girl in the hospital;
and bought your own class ring.

It's true you didn't save much money,
but I was always so proud of you;
You paid for your own expenses:
pictures, gowns, and other things, too.

We had many a battle,
and even one big fight;
But I always loved you, Sandy,
and you learned what was right.

It was amazing how well you did in school
while working six days a week;
You learned that money didn't grow on trees,
and you must work to get what you seek.

Think big, Sandy, the world is yours,
and you have the ability to go far;

JUST SET YOUR GOAL, have faith in God,
and you can reach a far-off star.

I know how thrilled you were,
when you were the football princess one day;
When you rode down the field looking so lovely,
"that's my daughter," I proudly did say.

Your life is just beginning,
although your high school days are through;
Thanks for being my daughter,
and I'm very proud of you.

Love, Mommy

To Bobo with Love

I wrote this poem June 4, 1971
For my second child's high school graduation.

Dear Bobo,

Graduation is here at last,
this is my gift for you tonight;
It's been a joy to be your mother,
and teach you wrong from right.

As a newborn baby, you were so loud,
you cried night and day;
Time went so fast — soon it was cub scouts,
and you were on your way.

You had lots of fun growing up —
picnic, swimming, and a "hours in a tree";
Family parties — Uncle Art singing,
"The Little Shirt That Mother Made For Me."

Bike hikes, camping in the woods,

and catching fish down at " Crows Run."
Playing baseball out in the field,
many hours in the hot summer sun.

Little league was a treat,
you got trophies and felt like a star;
You worked as a janitor in 5th grade,
saving money for a car.

I thought to myself, what a dreamer,
not with that little money he made;
But you bought your car when you were fifteen,
and every penny you paid.

Daddy helped you work on it,
and finally, the engine sounded good;
You washed, waxed, and cared for that car,
and learned what was under the hood.

You worked summers cutting grass,
and scrubbed many a hospital floor;
You learned the value of money,
and were prepared for things life had in store.

High school — You were so happy, football and basketball,
you did you very best;
You weren't the greatest star,
but, You had more spirit than all the rest.

Football camp, teenage parties,
many memories to keep
"There is No Place Like Home,"
the picture in your room where you sleep.

I know deep in your heart,
pro baseball is a dream you wish would come true;
But, hang in there, Bo, keep the faith,
and remember God has great plans for you.

You never had a fancy home,
or money in great amount;
But, you have been over-supplied
with spiritual blessings that count.

OFF to college you soon will go —
Bo, give it all you can give;
You can help make this world,
a better place in which to live.

When we all sit around the table and say,
"Our God is Great";
I know I'll feel a little sad,
that there is one less plate.

Bobo, you are a born leader,
thoughtful, special, and kind;
And I thank God so many times
that you are a son of mine.

Love, Mom

My Son - Charlie

Charlie is a Mesing guy;
he got along well in school.
He played sports like all the rest,
but he was nobody's fool.

He seemed just like a quarterback
when he played on the basketball floor.
His fellow players watched him closely,
as he helped to build the score.

Hustle, Hustle , down the court —
mouth as dry as cotton — got to win the game.
Push yourself, give it all you got —
Give old Freedom High a good name.

When it came to high man for basketball points,
Charlie was always behind.
But, he had many basket assists,
and one one of the best players you could find.

In Little League Baseball, he was a star,

and a catcher by name.
Charlie could really swing a bat,
and helped the team to win a game.

A baseball marked "Grand Slam, 6-13-67"
still sits on our dresser today.
I remember that homerun — and others —
Oh, how I loved to watch him play.

He was no great lover of football,
but, he played and did his part.
He was a careful football player, made MAC team,
but football wasn't in his heart.

I remember watching Charlie in a school play,
he played Uncle Ben.
"Death of a Salesman" — was the play —
god acting — we applauded now and then.

After graduation,
he searched to find what life had in store.
He graduated from college,
and life opened for him a new door.

He marries his beloved Cana,
and they were happy as man and wife.
But he is still sometimes searching,
for a change now and then in his life.

Oh how I love that Charlie,
and I'll love him 'till I die.
He has made me so proud and happy,
and he is "The apple of my eye."   November 5, 1981

4

Bobby – The Positive Thinker

Many people of today are negative thinking
and live life with very little fun;
But I know a young man who is a positive thinker,
and that is Bobby, my son.

If by chance you talk to him,
and listen to him explain a dream;
You can feel the "positive thinking" within him,
and you will understand what I mean.

This last year has had some hard times,
not knowing where to go,Or what to do;
But he has gained much knowledge and experience,
And shared some beautiful memories too.

He knows some sorrows that one can feel,
and trials that happen in life;
He knows the lonely-empty-feeling of heartache,
from being without his beloved wife.

Written by: Doris Mesing

But environment causes people to change -
sometimes life becomes a race;
After four short of marriage, Bobby,
maybe it's time to change your pace.

I remember how excited and scared you were;
you showed Daddy your plan, & explained what you wanted to do;
Being a "positive thinker", Bobby,
you built that log cabin, and shared a dream or two.

Within a very short time, your losses were great;
You lost your home, your job, and also lost your mate.
But life goes on, "All Things Pass,"
And we discover God is still very near;

You still have your darling daughter, Rachel,
And can still fulfill a dream without fear.

Don't have a sour outlook on marriage, Bobby,
It takes two working hard from the very start;
God believes in marriage!
Don't judge it, from the bad scar left in your heart.

With the help of God and your loved ones,
and a few more dreams to fulfill,
You will find happiness and peace,
Because you are a "positive thinker" still.

Love, Mom
July 16, 1981

5

Linda – Your Special Graduation Day

Yesterday, May 29, was a day to remember — your graduation from Penn State.

You have studied and worked real hard — you won't forget that date.

Your four years of college have been a struggle — sometimes funds were low.

You were always working, paying for your education — learning how to grow.

Your first two years of college — six semesters — Daddy only paid for one.

You were so thankful for that K-Mart job — you had little time for fun.

Then you worked at college, that cafeteria job sometimes made you sweat.

How grateful you were for that J&L summer job —and steel workers you met.

Although you have been rejected from Grad School — things are not the same.

You will get your chance for higher learning — you will "play the game".

Written by: Doris Mesing

We all remember- May 29 - and the fun we had with your friends that day.

College has had many happy times — sometimes you wish that you could stay.

You will miss your Kurt, Cathy Mike, and also friends like Don, too.

But the world is full of friends, Linda — and many more for you.

You gave memories to treasure — like the time you danced ,till "soaked-wet".

"We Are Family", dancing in a circle — you have many dreams to gather yet.

Keep your goal within your heart — I wish you happiness, Love, and fame.

You are a special person to us at home — Good Luck — as you "Play the Game"

Love, Mom

Sunday, May 30, 1982

6

George – My Youngest Son

One day I realized my youngest son
was growing too fast for me;
So I wrote this poem —this was in July 1972

Sweet little George,
only eight years old
Sweet little George,
stories I've told.

I miss my little boy,
he is growing so fast;
I held him on my lap,
and read him stories in the past.

Now he reads his own stories,
and he runs out the kitchen door;
Always on the go,
baseball glove laying on the floor.

Riding on his orange bicycle,
many hours at the swimming pool.
He loves his new muscle shirt
and thinks he is cool.

I hardly ever get a hug,
he is too busy for me;
He has his secret cabins
and things I cannot see.

Enjoy your childhood, little George,
you still have time to grow;
I am just a mother watching you,
and oh, "I love you so!"

7

The Home Wreckers

Grandchildren

Sandy is the mother
Bumper is the dad;
At first, two little home wreckers,
were all that we had.

God smiled and them,
and soon there were more;
The homewreckers are our grandchildren,
who run through the kitchen door.

Bobby and Diana have one so far,
Rachel is her name;
She is a beautiful little girl,
but, a home wrecker just the same.

The homewreckers run through the house,
messing it up as they go;
But Gram and Pap don't mind,
because the kids set their hearts aglow.

These grandchildren give us
happiness, love, and joy;
thank God our Father,
for every little girl and boy.

1977

Fathers Day

Happy Father's Day to you John, it's your special day;
I hope you will enjoy it, my love, and are happy in every way.

You have six kids that love you, and a wife who loves you, too.
God has been good to all of us and will continue to bless you.

So be happy on Father's Day, the world will keep us turning;
With God as your director, we will keep on learning.

Father's Day this Sunday, will be a day o'clock and rest;
You are a good father, John, and we think you are the very best.

June 14, 1977

Johnny - the Soldier

This poem was written in 1946 when I was in 10th grade.

J — Is for the journey, which he is now on
O— is for the ocean, on which he'll come back to me someday.
H — is for home, which is every soldier's dream.
N — is for never will I stop loving him, it seems.
N — is for his name, which is a wonderful sound to me;
Y — is for his youth, and he's as cute as can be.

If you put all these letters together, that I have written above;
You'll see that they spell Johnny, the guy I really love.

Forty Thousand Dollars

If I had forty thousand dollars, you know what I would do?
I'd invest it in US Bonds, and save it all for, you.

I'd ration it out to us, over a period of a year or four;
I'd figure it out, so that when someone came to the door.

We'd have enough money to pay our bills, and each special need;
We'd buy a little tractor, and buy a little seed.

Then, my love, you could retire, and you could chase a dream;
You could sail, at peace, down life's happy endless stream.

If I had forty thousand dollars, what happiness it could bring;
But, forget it friend, I'm rich enough, I have a wedding ring.

A Chipper's Wife
1960

John – The One I Love

I wrote this poem for my husband in December 1978

We have been together, John,
for over thirty years;
We have had some great times,
and you have helped to calm my fears;

We both have made mistakes and hurt each other,
this is true,
But, we are still together,
and the sun is shining through.

You have always been my love,
friend, consciousness, and my guide;
In your own way,
you saved my life and gave me back my pride.

There was a time in your life
when you had a great personality change;
You thought we should part,
and our lives, we should rearrange.

I thought that I would lose you,
my heart ached, and I cried;
But, little then did I know,
this time would strengthen me inside.

We stayed together during this unhappy time,
and I wondered what would be;
But I slowly got myself together,
and now I am a different me.

We've shared many fond memories,
and I am happy to be your wife;
You've helped me more than you will ever know,
to have some direction in my life.

I love you John, my darling,
you are very important to me;
Thank you for helping me over "life's rough road,"
thanks for setting me FREE.

12

My Ideal Man

*This poem was accepted for publication in the
Anthology of High School Poetry,
National Association; School Days, 1946*

My ideal man has blond hair and dreamy blue eyes;
I think he is wonderful, and I will never tell him lies.

He doesn't drink, and sometimes he doesn't smoke;
I don't know why, but he's never broke.

He is a perfect gentleman, where ever he goes;
What makes him so wonderful, nobody knows.

His shirt is always tucked in, and his pants are always pressed;
In school, no matter what he does, he always does his best.

This is my ideal man, he is at the top of my list;
The only trouble is, he doesn't even exist.

The Treasures of My Life

The treasures of my life have flown away,
and only one son remains at the nest
Soon, he too will test his wings, go out in the world,
and try to be the best.

God blessed me with six children,
they will be the treasures of my life;
They have filled my years with
happiness, hope, love, sorrow, and sometimes even strife.

The love I feel for each of them is strong,
different, and sometimes even new.
It is the love a mother feels toward her children,
they are her chosen few.

Although each child is different,
I cannot say who will be the best.
They all have God within their hearts,
some more outstanding in traits, one as good as the rest.

There is no special daughter, there is no special son,
the six will always be equal, love has made them one.

Although their lives change year by year,
opportunities will continue to be at their door.
They make mistakes, have good and happy times,
live and learn, and I love them as before.

Thank you God Almighty, for my children,
and for all the things for them which you have done;

May they never take your Love lightly, but be forever grateful,
and know that you alone are NUMBER ONE.

February 21, 1981

14

Mother

When I was a tiny baby, and used to fret and cry;
Mom always came to feed me, and saw that I was dry.

From her, I learned many things, at Elan months I could walk;
She taught me to feed and dress myself, and gave me the gift of talk.

I short blond hair, bangs, and bright blue eyes;
Mom always loved me, even when I told little lies.

Finally I grew up, and went to first grade in school;
I enjoyed the school picnics, and fun at the swimming pool.

She took me to Sunday School and Church, and taught me to be nice;
She made me pretty dresses, and for me made many a sacrifice;

I just lived for Christmas and Easter, they were my biggest thrill;
Mom made these all possible, and I wish I were a kid still.

I remember when I was in the hospital, I waited for visiting hours;
Mom would come to visit me, she was like sunshine and flowers.

Mom is sweet, wonderful, lots of fun, and kind;
If I searched this whole world over, a better friend I couldn't find.

Can she cook — umm I should surely say;
She can make the best food, and mix it any old way.

She makes life worth living, without her, there wouldn't be a home;
It's the nicest place in the world, no matter how far you may roam.

Everything I have or shall have, I know I owe to no other;
She's so understanding and wise, and really a perfect mother.

1946

15

Living in Paradise

Life in the 1940s

We get up at eleven each morning,
after our breakfast in bed;
Get ready for school about noon,
bedecked in sweaters of red.

First period is a study hall,
with plenty of laughter and talk;
Period two is a health class,
we all go out for a walk;

Then to the gym when the bell rings,
for a ballgame the rest of the day;
We parade through the halls at our leisure,
chewing bubblegum all the way.

At four to the lunchroom we travel,
to get strawberry sundaes for free!!
The school is a paradise perfect,
as anyone can plainly see.

After our delicious sundaes,
our work for the day is done;
All aboard on the school bus for movies,
then home for an evening of fun.

.

Now, if you envy this picture of life
at Moon Township High School;
There is really one thing certain,
and that is: "April Fool."

John and Baseball.

I wrote this poem for a man named John Genova,
Who loved kids and baseball.
I read it to all the parents and boys who were at a baseball picnic
at the end of the season at Brady's Run Park, in August 1970.

It has been many years,
but it seems like only yesterday;
Since you took our little boys,
and taught them how to play.

We remember "minor league",
how they would jump to strike at the ball;
Sometimes there were two on base,
and they never heard the umpire call!

Then came "major league,"
and they learned how to win a game;
You taught them much about baseball,
and slowly led them to fame.

It was so much fun to play baseball,
but what a thrill to win!
You taught them more than baseball,
as you coached them, time again.

Pony league was great —
some of the boys were champs there;
Your boys loved and respected you,
not one who didn't care.

Colts came next for the boys,
the urge to win was strong;
You showed them their mistakes,
and told them when they were wrong.

But, they are champs for you, John,
and every parent here;
We're proud of you and our boys,
to us they are very dear.

Baseball is really wonderful,
as our God looks down from above;
I'm sure that He is thanking you, John,
for all your baseball love.

17

Football

Summer is almost over, school time is getting near;
Now it's time to start the season, football camp is here.

Boys are happy, full of pep —determined to win come what may;
But, as the practice roughs them up, they droop at the end of the day.

They come home thirsty, they really don't want to eat;
They ache in every muscle — and are exhausted from the heat.

But, they survive the first week, and all pass the test;
Then go for another week, determined to do their best.

Football mothers are busy, there is much to do;
They plan for the season, and help with camp meals and snacks, too.

The boys come home all enthused — they know it won't be long;
Soon they will be able to prove — that their team is very strong.

Dirty socks!! Smelly shirts! Will those practice suits come clean?
Mothers do their part, helping a son fulfill a dream.

Written by: Doris Mesing

When football camp is over, it will be remembered by each boy;
Although it has been very rough, there have been moments of joy.

Out they run, on to the field! Ready to win their first game;
A football hero they want to be — life is not the same.

Each mother is in the stand, says a silent prayer;
Even on the football field, God is surely there.

Sept 1970

Sandys Wedding day

*This poem was written for my oldest daughter
on her wedding day, May 6, 1972.*

Congratulations to the bride and groom,
this is your wedding day;
Sandy and Bumper,
you probably think that happiness is here to stay.

But, life will bring some problems,
some things will be hard to take;
You will feel you are floating on a cloud,
as you cut your wedding cake.

Your marriage will be strengthened,
if you worship together as man and wife;
The little fights will easily be forgotten,
if God is in the center of your life.

Money is a marriage trap,
so handle it with care;
You'll be amazed how it stretches,
when you give the Lord his share.

Your blessings now are many,
your marriage has a good start;
Remember that it pays,
to have a forgiving heart.

God will continue to bless you,
as you live side by side;
Your marriage will blossom and bloom,
with Jesus Christ as your guide.

Love, Mom

19

Prince of Peace

This is a poem I wrote to my son, Bo,
during a time in his life while he was a follower of the Maharaji,
and lived in a commune for five years.
He believed the Maharaji was the messiah of today.

Dear Bo,

Never think it was a waste of money,
that you made your visit home;
It was a real treat for all of us, and please return,
no matter where you may roam.

We have accepted the fact
that you are a truly dedicated man;
So you must follow your own heart, Bo,
and continue with God's plan.

I am taking your advice,
and meditation will be a part of my life;
For now I realize that an inner light
is a part of the struggle of life.

So be happy, Bo, and know that God
wants you to have peace, love, and joy;
I realize that you have grown past your years,
and you are no longer a boy.

I will always love you, Bo —
with a mother's love that will never cease;
In my heart, you will always remain;
My true PRINCE OF PEACE.

Love Mom
January 8, 1976

20

Thank You Mrs. Stitch

I read this poem and presented it to Mrs. Stitch
at a special program for the girl scouts in the
New Sewickley Township Presbyterian Church on May 16, 1971.

We went to visit a theater,
for some of us, it was our first real play;
We really enjoyed the acting,
and hearing what the actors had to say.

In the winter we went ice skating,
this was a real treat;
It was plenty cold, but we had fun,
also many cold feet.

We enjoyed the bus trip to "Old McConnell's Mill",
also the hike on the trail;
We had a really gay time roller-skating,
and sometimes, many of us fell.

We even enjoyed selling candy, and articles,
for our trip this June;
We are looking forward to Cedar Point,
and hope the time will come soon.

We had a good time swimming,
and this we did for free;
Girl Scouts has been great this year,
fun for you and me.

We owe a lot to our leader,
and we feel so very rich;
That we have for you for our leader,
Thank you, Mrs. Stitch.

A Football Mothers Prayer

Be with us Heavenly Father, as we meet for every plan;
Guide us and direct us, by your almighty hand.

Be with our football players, in each and every game;
They are so very special, not just a number or a name.

When we work as football parents, give us that "heartfelt" joy;
Knowing that we have added to the happiness of some boy.

Thank You, God our Father, as you shower your gifts from above;
Guide each and every player, may he learn to feel your love.

Sept 1971

THANK YOU, BARBARA

Fourteen sessions ago,
we came to study "As Christians Teach";
We came as "eager beavers",
our pupils we wanted to reach.

We studied "Why We Teach",
learning often means to "change";
"We must know each pupil",
and our classes we will rearrange.

When the learner becomes a "witness",
Christian education is right;
A "learning experience" is helpful;
the "objective" we must keep in sight.

The teacher becomes a part of the pupil,
at times we must be quiet, too;
Learning is best when pupils are involved;
this is important to do.

We studied making bulletin boards;
a good way to break the ice;
Then those group discussions,
sometimes weren't very nice.

Age group studies' case studies,
made the wheels in our brains turn;
The records of a class in session,
rap sessions, all helped us to learn.

Then the study of a "picture",
one without a name;
When it came to personal opinions,
they were never all the same.

Role plays, dramatic reading,
"Rosetta and Joseph", are memories to keep;
These are the ways to learn the Scriptures,
they help us to dig deep!

Keep in practice Barbara,
the Lord needs teachers like you;
You have guided and helped us change,
our outlook is different, too.

Many thanks and good wishes,
from all of us who are here;
We had fun, and learned as well,
"Thank you Barbara, dear."

23

Dear Heavenly Father

I spent many happy times with the girl scouts.
At camp, once we did a skit of Noah and his ark.
Bumper, my son-in-law, drew us a large picture of the ark.,
Which we p[laced in the background against the wall.
I wrote this prayer to give, in our closing devotions,
just before we left for home.
Read by Connie Jordan.

Thank you for this weekend, from every Girl Scout here;
It has been fun and joy, and we felt that you were near.

Some cooking, singing and dancing, and other pleasures, too;
With other girl scouts all around, we had much to do.

We're all packed and ready to leave, soon we'll be on our way;
But our memories we'll keep, as we leave this Sabbath Day.

Winter Camp, 1972

24

Place Up on the Hill

Mengel Heights

I wrote the poem below when I was in An inspired mood with God
January 1975

One day there was an empty spot,
high upon a hill;
And God decided he would build,
a community for His will.

These people were so happy,
they could see far below;
How nice it was to live up there,
many things they did not know.

It wasn't easy to get supplies,
but the scenery was grand.
The people felt so close to God,
they lived hand in hand.

Even today, when we go real high,
we can see some wonderful sights;
And we know that God has blessed and preserved.

Freedom's Mengel Heights.

25

Autumn

I wrote this for my sister Retz, in October 1975

Mornings are starting to get very cold;
autumn is coming, a story to be told.

Pumpkins in a garden, colored leaves everywhere;
We are looking forward to the day that Halloween is here.

The smell of autumn, with leaves flying around;
Boys playing football - tumbling on the ground.

We'll have some warm days and we'll enjoy them all.
Autumn is a great time, thank you, God for the season of fall.

26

The Butterfly Lady -
Dorothy

The beautiful "Butterfly Lady",
sits at her desk each day;
She is a real credit to Jefferson Trace,
and she knows what to say.

She adds something to the office,
her looks, her manner, her smile;
One look at the clothes she wears,
and you'll know that she has style.

It is not always easy,
she gets different complaints day after day;
But she has the ability,
and she handles them in the proper way.

The cleaning ladies respect her,
as she gives them orders to go "trucking along";
She never expects too much,
but she will tell you when you are wrong.

The butterfly is a symbol to her,
she had to struggle during a hard part of life to live;
Now, she is a beautiful, well adjusted person,
with much in life to give.

I'm glad I met you "Butterfly Lady",
your memory will stay;
You seem so full of happiness and life,
and you smile like you could just fly away.

January 19, 1980

27

Billy and Bill

This poem was read at the farewell church luncheon given
for Billy and Bill Jung, before they left for Florida. Sunday May 25, 1980.

You have been a part of our church family,
for so many years;
You have shared so many good times,
and also we have shed some tears.

The "Friendship Guild" was a part of your life,
Billy you knew what to do;
The ladies, and also the pastors,
knew they could count on you.

The banquets, dinners, and our kitchen,
all knew your special touch;
We leaned on you Billy,
you served us well, and gave us so much.

The friendship and love we have shared,
from Trinity Prince of Peace;
Will always be remembered,
and our church family love will never cease.

We know you love your church Bill,
as financial secretary, you did your part;
The men of the church, and the pastors,
knew that you had a willing heart.

Some of us remember watching as Chook and Dick grow,
an important part in your life;
Your children made you proud of them,
with very little strife.

We have gathered together around our Communion Table,
with family love, year after year;
There will always be a bond between us,
you are special people and we care.

We have memories to share with you,
some are happy, and some are blue;
Thank you Billy and Bill,
for letting us share a part of our life with you.

28

Jim – The Maintenance Man

Jim is the maintenance man,
he works at Jefferson Trace;
He gets calls constantly,
he keeps a steady pace.

When a cleaning lady hears a sound,
that seems to come from nowhere;
That means that Jim with his radio
is around and very near.

His radio is always tuned in –
in his pocket and his truck;
Many tenants depend on Jim,
without his assistance, they would be stuck.

He is "Mr. Fix It", he answers requests,
no matter how big or small;
He is over supplied with special knowledge,
and he answers many a call.

The ladies seem to love him,
and are glad he is around;
The men depend on him too,
and listen for his radio sound.

Jim is a credit to Jefferson Trace,
and he does the best he can;
He is really kind of special;
some call him the "Miracle Man".

November 23, 1980

29

Happy Birthday Gusty

Happy Birthday Gusty,
from each and every one.
We have been together many years
and have had lots of fun.

We'll always remember the many years
that you took time to teach;
We'll remember Reverend Roeck
and how some of us called him "Preach."

Many good times in the friendship guild,
you were always apart;
Ladies Aid, and other groups,
you helped us to get a start.

The children came you taught them,
they grew and went away;
But many of the Sunday School children,
kept your lessons in their heart to stay.

Summer picnics, cornrows,
close feelings at Christmas and Easter time.
You are always a part of us,
and I was glad that you were a friend of mine.

May you have many more happy years,
here at the Prince of Peace;
we all love you gusty
and may that love and friendship never cease.

February 8 1981

30

A Wedding Poem for Lisa and Timmy

I wrote this poem for my neighbor's grandson
on his wedding day, July 24 1981.

Good luck Lisa and Timmy,
for you have much to share;
You have the gift of love
and each other to care.

Sometimes life seems unfair,
and you don't know where to turn;
But, if you take time, have patience,
there was much you can learn;

Your friends and family will love you,
no matter how bad times may seem;
Don't be afraid Timmy and Lisa,
plan and make a real dream;

The happiness you share with your baby
is a true symbol of your love.
Material things are least important,
you have been blessed with "God's Grace" from above.

31

Happy Anniversary – Dot and Joe

I wrote this for my neighbor's 25th Wedding Anniversary

Happy anniversary from all your friends and family
that are here tonight;
Twenty five good years,
and your marriage has been right.

Some times were very happy,
and sometimes are very sad;
But you were always together,
to share the good and the bad.

It seems only yesterday,
Joey was a little boy, climbing a tree;
Now he's a fine young man,
and you are as proud as can be.

Then there were the twins, playing in shorts,
life was hectic when there were four.
Now to handsome football players,
Ron and Don, walked through your kitchen door.

Davey is still growing,
and loves to play baseball;
Then there is pretty Linda,
who hates to be called Doll.

There were times when work was not,
but the garden always grew.
You two canned vegetable soup,
and there was much to do.

Finally the house was paid,
and there was a new car;
You had many happy years,
and you will still go far.

"Good luck Dot and Joe,"
Happy Anniversary, we wish you the very best;
God has showered you with blessings,
and you are surely blessed.

32

Life

What is our goal in life; is it wealth, happiness, or fame?
Do we love our neighbor, live in Christ, no matter what the game?

There is only one God, we must believe this is true;
He is The One all around us, who watches us the whole day through.

We often try to keep up with the Jones, that is material wise;
But, we should try to love, and live in God's eyes.

Heaven will be wonderful, many of our loved ones we will see;
We hope and pray and wonder, is there room up there for me.

1970

33

Easter Sunday

Easter Sunday is a happy time, we wish it were here to stay;
We all know that Christ is living and that he leads the way.

We all must do our duty, whatever it may be;
If we want to share, in the life of eternity.

When we slip and fall and get off the track,
We need to get close to God, He can bring us back.

If we want to share in His rich reward, this is the story told;
We must have salvation, in order to get the pot of gold.

The sun will always shine, but Easter comes only once a year;
Let us live in peace and love for him, our Jesus dear

April 2, 1972

34

I Thank You - God

I wrote this poem for a Nun named "Sister Maryann."
She was my favorite teacher while I was a student nurse doing
my psychiatric serve at St Francis Hospital in Pittsburgh 1949.

I thank you God, for my voice to sing;
I thank you God for my everything.
For a nice home, and a swell mom and dad;
for everything good, that I ever had.

For the ability to reason, remember and learn;
for the sky, sea, and sweet-smelling fern.
For the pleasure I get, while caring for the sick,
and for the thrill I feel inside when I see a newborn baby kick.

For the happy days and nights, of moonlight and flowers;
For all the friends I have, my family, and many happy hours.
For all things I enjoy and love, whether great or small,
These are the things I thank you for, I thank you for them all.

35

My Little Sunshine Girl

Rachel

I have a little sunshine girl,
and Rachel is her name;
She longs to hug her mommy,
but this world is not the same.

She lives in Texas far away,
and I cannot hold her anymore.
She is only five years old,
and I wonder what is in store;

I am only her grandmother,
and I long to see her smile.
Her mind is sometimes in darkness,
she stays with her daddy a while.

I hope that God will help my Sunshine Girl,
to understand someday;
That mothers and daddies make mistakes,
but they still love her, even though, they may be miles away.

36

Football Memories

Tonight is the last football game of the season
and I'm feeling a little sad
George is playing his last football game
and I'm anything but glad

The Mesings have given for football players
to good old Freedom High
there was Bobo Charlie Bobby
and now George finishes with a sigh

Bobo wasn't the greatest football player
but in High Spirits he was far ahead
he usually played the monster man
and if given the chance he could knock them dead

Charlie was a careful player
who did his best to avoid a sack
he was a good player and
won a Mac award - a shining football plaque.

Bobby was so darling
he would plow right through the line
as I watched him playing football
I thought Bobby you are doing fine.

Yes George is playing his last football game
for good old Freedom High
He'll have some happy football memories
As time goes passing by

the wind is strong and the air is cold
and we have a tough team to play to play tonight
but win or lose you better believe
Freedom will give New Brighton a fight.

Tonight while I watch my youngest son play in the game
I'll probably shed a tear now and then
Remembering my four football players
and all the football memories that have been

Doris November 6th 1981

37

The Crimson Lady – A Volunteer Worker

Today I'll visit the Geriatric Center,
and see what my ladies have to say.
I usually visit five of them;
and they help to brighten my day.

They are so happy to have a visitor;
they give a big hello and smile.
I sit down and sometimes read,
or just chat and laugh a while.

When I first met Mary she was quiet,
sad and close to tears;
She seldom got any visitors,
and she had been there for over 30 years.

Mary is a little retarded but,
she was so happy to have a visitor near,
She began to laugh and smile at times,
but I had to shout so she could hear.

My ladies are mostly over eighty;
vision and hearing are a problem, and Mildred is blind.
I read her the guideposts stories,
and she is so very grateful to me, and also very kind.

Thalia's eyes are very red and watery,she says she cannot read today.
I give her a large print magazine,and read a poem before I go away

Ruth grabs my arm and hugs me,as I walk over to her wheelchair.
She is so happy to see me,she says she knows I care.

Ruth wants to sing a song today,
but an eighty-eight year old lady, needs help if she is to sing.
So I helped her sing "In The Garden", and she is smiling,
and I can see the happiness I can bring.

I tried to bring some sunshine to all the ladies;
I smile and let them know I care.

Rose is so happy when I write her notes,
because she is deaf and cannot hear.
She says she cannot read lips, but has good eyesight.
Rose is so happy when we communicate, and I take time to write.

When my visiting time is over at the Geriatric Center,
And I walk out the door, my heart begins to sing.
Today, I've made someone happy - I'm just a "Crimson Lady",
and happy to be doing my thing

December 1981

38

My Favorite Place

There is a place within her home which is very dear to me.
I love to spend much time here is my dearest place to be.

The floor is pretty and shiny; the cupboards I love them all.
A rocking chair sits in the corner, for friends that come to call.

My sewing machine is in this place, I used it many a day.
My typewriter is my heart's delight, it is here to stay.

I love to cook in my kitchen the counters are a joy to behold.
I love the pretty walls and space to me it's worth more than gold.

Oh how I love my kitchen, here many a letter I write.
Johnny made this room for me, it is my "Heart's Delight".

February 17th 1982

39

Christmas Memories

This poem won an award it was printed in
The Beaver Valley Times December 24th 1981

The children are sitting at the table
with spoons in their little hands.
Helping mother to ice Christmas cookies
talking about Santa's plans.

The Christmas tree is trimmed,
the children smile with delight.
All six are so excited,
they heart they can hardly wait for tonight.

Mother hurries with supper dishes,
it's been it has been a busy day.
It is Christmas Eve
and time for the children's Christmas play.

The Sunday best clothes are ready,
with help they all get dressed.
Tonight while up in front of the church,
they will do their very best.

The Christmas tree inside the church
helps to make the children able,
To realize "True Christmas"
and Jesus born in a stable.

Presents and boxes of candy,
make the children laugh with joy.
They know this is a time to celebrate
the birth of a baby boy.

After the Christmas program is over,
home we go and ready for bed.
They all gather round Mother,
as once more the Christmas story is read.

Midnight candlelight service,
then getting the presents under the tree;
What a great feeling at Christmas time,
it's good to be just me.

Now the six children are all grown
and some have moved away and gone.
But I thank God many times
for my Christmas Memories that Linger on.

December 1981

40

Big Wyoming

A few miles from Riverton Wyoming,
sets a trailer on seven acres of dust.
Times were hard in Pennsylvania,
so The Parkers move was a must.

At times the money was low,
but the rewards of Wyoming are great.
It is a land of natural beauty and wealth,
a very special State.

There is a dream for the Parkers,
to have trees all over their land;
The irrigation rights will help,
they'll find a way to make a stand.

When the interest rates go down,
and the economy takes an upward swing,
Maybe the Parkers will build a house,
and be happy doing their thing.

Bumper is a good provider,
with fish, antelope, elk and deer;
He loves this hunting land,
and is glad the mountains are near.

Big Wyoming has many Treasures -
Thermopolos Hot Springs, is not too far away;
Then there is Yellowstone National Park,
a place where visitors would love to stay.

Thank you God for big Wyoming,
keep my beloved Parker's safely in your care;
That they may find happiness and peace within your state,
this will be my prayer

April 6th 1982

41

A Need for Love

I need someone to smile at me when I walk through the door;
I need someone who is in love with me, like a love I had before.

To have someone to talk to me, and looked me in the eye;
Someone, when he leaves the house, will stop and kiss me goodbye.

One cannot force a person to love them, something I have learned;
Sometimes I'm growing impatient when my love is not returned.

I hope my darling will love me again, I need his love every day;
I'll keep on trying to win him back, God will hear me when I pray.

May 8th 1982

42

Rose

There is a lady named Rose,
who's just in the same spot each day;
She sits on the sun porch, in the Geriatric Center,
and has good things to say.

She reads her prayers each morning,
and for me, she always has a smile;
I write her notes because she is deaf,
and we communicate for a while.

Rosa is always cheerful
and her smile is always bright;
She doesn't complain,
though she sits in her wheelchair from morning 'til night.

I'm glad that I met you Rose,
sometimes you help to brighten my day;
You are a friend and I want to keep -
a friend and I want to stay

October 1982

Our Thanksgiving Day

Thank you God our Father for this Special Day;
As we gather here together, hear us as we pray.

Our blessings still are many, though fear is all around;
You are our Salvation God, please don't let your whole world down.

Thank you for the joy and comfort, that Daddy and Desta now share;
Thank you for their families and all their friends that care.

As we eat this Thanksgiving meal, we all want you to know;
We are forever thankful God, that you have made it so

November 25th 1982

Christmas Eve 1982

Christmas Eve 1982 was a real treat that night;
Three of our six children were home and things seemed really bright.

The house just glowed with Christmas, and Christmas in the air;
The house, once lonely, was alive with people that really cared.
We dressed for church and went to candlelight services to pray;
We sang and felt so close to God, and will remember that day.

As we stood together in the darkened church,
and sang silent night with our candles all aglow
We had much to be thankful for and;
We knew our feeling for God would surely grow.

Charlie George and Linda were all present that Christmas Eve;
Then there was Canna, Jolene, John, and I, and we all did believe.
So Christmas Eve 1982 has a special memory in my heart;
I'll cherish it long as I live - 3 children are here to share a part.

December 26th 1982

45

The Blue Bird

Pretty little blue bird sitting by my door;
Sitting pretty little bluebird, who are you looking for?

John has built a bird feeder, so eat as much as you can;
I hear you singing Bluebird, are you afraid of man?

Before too long spring will come and you will build a nest;
We hope you choose one of our birdhouses they are the very best.

Fly around little blue bird, but don't go too far away;
We like to watch you and hear you sing, and we hope you will stay.

December 31st 1982

46

Bumper

Bumper was tall and Bumper was strong;
Bumper thought Wyoming was like a song.

He loves the mountains and also every plane;
He loves to fish and also hunt for game.

Wyoming was his spot, he decided here to live;
He found the peace in Wyoming, and he had much to give;

Bumper had dreams for his family,
but sometimes dreams are changed;
Sandy is the head of the household now, things will be rearranged.

I can still see him dive in the water, what a perfect dive;
Bumper's memory would be with us always, like when he was alive.

Thank you, God, our Creator,
for giving Bumper the things he loved best;
We know that his Spirit belongs to you,
he has found Eternal rest.   August 28th 1983

The Treasures of
My Life

The treasures of my life have flown away,
and only one son remains at the nest;
Soon he too will test his wings,
go out into the world and try to be the best.

God has blessed me with 6 children,
they will always be the treasures of my life;
They have filled my years with happiness,
hope, love, sorrow, and sometimes even strife.

The love I feel for each of them is strong,
different, and sometimes even new;
It is the love a mother feels toward her children,
they are her Chosen Few.

Although each child is different,
I cannot ever say who will be the best;
They all have God within their hearts,
some more outstanding in traits, one as good as the rest;

There is no special Daughter
and there is no special Son;
The six will always be equal,
Love has made them as One.

Although life changes year by year,
opportunities will continue to be at their door;
They make mistakes, have good and happy times,
live and learn; and I love them as before.

Thank you God Almighty, for my children
and for all the things for them you have done;
May they never take your love lightly,
but be forever grateful and know that you are NUMBER ONE.

February 21, 1981

Sandy is Home

My daughter Sandy and her husband Bumper and four children, moved from PA to Wyoming, seeking work.

Bumper was killed shortly after, in a trucking accident.

Sandy roughed it for two years, with only the kids;

And then she and the family all moved back to PA to live.

They lived with us for 7 months then she got a Ryan home

Sandy is Home

Sandy is Home

From the kitchen, I hear a noise and see hugs and kisses galore;
A station wagon, kids all around, Dustin just ran through the door.

The Parkers are here from Wyoming why did they ever roam?
Everyone is happy, at last, Sandy has come home.

Bicycles that laid in the shed, are fixed and now on the road;
Look how happy Dustin is, he has just found a toad.

Dirty fingerprints on the door, things are scattered all around;
But who cares, Sandy is home, and now there is a new sound.

The five Parker's are here from Wyoming, and they are here to stay;
What happiness they are bringing, good times will come our way.

Laundry has no end, cooking and dishes galore;
But who cares, Sandy is home once more.

The once-empty house is alive and full as can be;
Things are different now – Sandy is home, you see.

Skin Deep

God made a little baby
and the color of her skin
was like a candle aglow;
The color of her skin
was one we did not know.

What is the color of your skin,
only God will know;
But what really counts,
is what is below.

Your skin may be beautiful,
soft as silk;
But God judges the inner beauty,
remember this when you choose a mate.

Doris Jan 1, 1986

The Wedding

Oh, happy wedding day we see;
When George and Joleen will marry.

The church bells will sound a time of cheer;
The happy wedding day is now here.

Our Lady of Peace, Joleen shall be;
In her own church, we will see.

A love united, strong, and great;
A love selected for each mate.

George has graduated and his employment is near;
Oh happy wedding day, it is one of love and care.

Mom August 15, 1986.

51

I Think of God

When the wind blows and the snow falls through the air,
I think of God.

When the freshly cut grass smells so good,
I think of God.

When I dive into a cool lake and swim like there is no end,
I think of God.

When I see little children playing in a park,
I think of God.

When I see a man working (no matter what kind),
I think of God.

When my husband holds me close, and I feel secure,
I think of God.

When I know there is life everlasting,
I know my God is real.   Doris August 16, 1986.

Later Bo

Tomorrow the sun will shine and you will leave our home;
Take care, my son, and keep the faith, wherever you may roam.

I hope that you find the dream that you have been searching for;
I hope happiness stays with you - you are like an "OPEN DOOR".

Remember who loves you the most in the world;
Remember who gave you life

God shall we reward you my son,
and soon you shall have a wife.

Love mom
August 8, 1986
Shortly after this poem, Bo found a wife.
Her name is Sri and she is from Indonesia
A real beautiful wife and worker.

53

Have You Paid Your Dues?

Have you paid your dues, to join the "Club of Man"?
It is a special club, you must work as hard as you can.

You must make someone smile, almost every day;
You must praise the Lord your God, be happy and gay.

You must touch someone you love and let them know you care;
You must hold on to a dream and learn what is fair;

Be thankful to God for each and everything;
Know and practice the thoughts that go with the wedding ring.

If you have paid your dues, friend, then this is what to do;
Just rejoice and be happy,
because "The Club of Man" is waiting for you!!!!

Heaven August 3, 1986.

54

The King is Home

The king is home, my son is home at last;
Bobo, you are a joy to my heart, but a sorrow to my past.

It is nice to have you home to visit with us again;
It is good to see you smile - that smile is for all men;

You are made of good stuff, and will always be a joy to me.
So go and get the WORLD Bo, and be as happy as you can be.

We know that you are SPECIAL,
Bo and there will never be another;
I am so proud of you
and happy to be your Mother

August 3, 1986 I love you Bo

55

George, From Valley Forge !!!

Get your act together, George the time is drawing near;
You are to become a leader and you need not fear.

The path has been made for you, follow it with care;
Just make a few Christian changes here and there.

You have chosen your own profession, let God lead your way.
I love you George and I will miss you what more can I say.

EXCEPT "LOOK OUT WORLD", George is here to stay.

Love mom August 4, 1986.

The K- Mart Queen

One day at a time, that is her secret, she will say;
She flies around giving orders, but she has her special way.

She is a gal who has her act together - you can plainly see;
She is a friend, an asset, and someone special to me.

Sandy leans on her, and she is the best we've seen;
This is Marlene Parker, and she is our Kmart queen.

Marlene is Bumper's Mother
Love to you - Doris
August 4, 1986.

Happy Birthday Daddy

Happy happy birthday,
and may you always be the same;
Happy happy birthday Daddy,
Red McClellan is your name.

All your kids still love you,
and we need you here;
Even though you've had some good times -
with mail pouch and beer.

We remember all the good times
that you have taken us through;
So happy happy birthday, Daddy,
happy birthday to you

August 12, 1986, your daughter Doris

The Children

They have all gone and flown away;
These are my children of yesterday

Sandy without her Bumper to care.
She does her best because the children are here.

Bo, home for a while, and learning to grow;
He's a produce man that the world should know.

Charlie is in Florida with talents galore;
All he needs is the right time to explore.

Linda still working hard trying to do her best;
Her time to shine is coming, and she will surprise all the rest.

Bobby has another dream, it includes some Montana land;
He is sick of traffic and people, he wants to make a new stand.

George is in college, trying to make a dream come true;
He will learn after trial and error, that there is much to do.

The house is sometimes lonely, with all the children so far away;
Sometimes they come to visit, but I know they cannot stay.

Bobby is out of Texas trying to make a dream come true.
George is at Penn State College, learning what chemical engineers do.

Hard times - good times - they do their best;
These are all my children, whom God has surely blessed.

Doris Mesing 1984

God Makes the Pretty Rainbows

God makes the pretty rainbows,
Away up in the sky;
It is a promise that he made to Noah
A promise for you and I.

When the sun is shining,
and it is raining, too;
The pretty rainbow comes out
and shines, for me and you.

God promised Noah he would never destroy
the earth with water again;
Now we have the promise -
our beautiful rainbows will glow for men.

Dedicated to Bobo 1986 Love Mom
He worked many years of the rainbow produce in Los Angeles

60

God

I heard your voice speak to me, a voice so good and kind;
Not a real loud or soft voice, but one in my mind.

It seems to whisper "I'm with you" it seems to say "I care".
When things are not right with me, I seem to feel you near.

The world may never change, and sometimes you seem so far away;
I wish I could be close to you, forever and a day.

I have so many blessings, I don't know where to start;
Many thanks to you - and I feel you deep within my heart.

Yes I know that you are real, God-loving good, and kind;
You're the voice I hear within me. you are often in my mind

1986

61

Happy Birthday Sandy

Happy birthday, Sandy, may it be your special day;
It has been a joy living with you, but now you must move away.

You need your own home and you need your freedom, too;
I can see you growing every day, and the Holy Spirit is within you.

I miss you when you are gone but you won't be going very far;
You'll be close when I need you, you'll be my guiding star.

Happy birthday Sandy, It really comes from the heart;
May God bless you forever, as you begin your life with a new start!

love Mom March 1986.

Flow Up the River of Life

Go up the river of life, the promised land is all around;
The water is fresh and blue, the waves hardly make a sound.

The fish here are gold and silver, and I love to watch them swim by;
The boats skim quietly across the water, I watch with a sigh;

A beautiful river of life, I could swim up your waters all day;
I could drink your wonderful water and be happy and gay.

Flow up the river of life, for God is present now you see;
As I flow up the river of life - I know this is the life for me.

Doris Mesing 1986
The Cold Springs of Florida and the many fish of silver and gold

63

Easter

Easter comes but once a year;
And when it comes, it brings good cheer;
We are thinking of spring, and warm sunshiny days;
We think of bunnies, jellybeans, and many happy ways.

We think of baked ham and families
together once more;
We think of Easter flowers
and Easter lilies galore.

We buy new clothes for church
and try to look as good as we can;
But most importantly,
we know that Easter is the time of the "Resurrected Man".

1986

64

I Can Still Dive

The water is cool, the water is clean;
Soon I'll know the thrill of a dive again.

I go down the steps, and swim to the end of the pool;
I pull myself up the ladder, near the dive.

Finally, out of the water, I walk over to the diving board;
Not looking back, I walk right out to the end of the diving board.

I am at the end of the diving board:
Feet together, hands together, to cut the water - body straight.

Splash !!! Down I go - what a thrill - a perfect dive!
My how good it feels to dive into that cool, clean water;

I swim like a fish under the water
The dive is over - up for air!!!

Doris 1986